Jess, Tom and Adam were friends.

Mrs Patel was their teacher.

It was playtime and Mrs Patel said,

'It's cold outside today.

Put your coats on and then you

can go out to play.'

The children went to get their coats.

1

'Here is my coat,' said Adam.
'Here is my coat,' said Jess.

'I can't see my coat,' said Tom.
'I can't go and play.'

3

'I will help you,' said Adam.
'Here is a coat.'

4

'This is not my coat,' said Tom.
'It is too big.'

'I will help you,' said Jess.
'Here is a coat.'

'This is not my coat,' said Tom.
'It is too little.'

'I can see my coat,' said Tom.

'Can you?' said Jess.

'This is my coat!' said Tom.

'And this is my coat!' said Jess.

'Now we can go and play,'
said Tom.